Flo and Ruby's Tail of Courage

Author: Shaz Ridler

Illustration and Art consultation: Chandrika Ariyasena & Jagath Kumara

Editor: Bandara Liyanage

Acknowledgements

I extend my heartfelt gratitude to Kathy for her unwavering encouragement, invaluable guidance, and steadfast support throughout the journey of bringing "Flo and Ruby's Remarkable Journey" to life. Your belief in this story has been a guiding light, and I am immensely thankful for your contributions.

A special thank you to Chrissy for entrusting me with little Ruby. It's an honour to have been able to bring Ruby's character to the pages of this book.

This book is dedicated to every child who faces moments of anxiety and uncertainty. Just like Flo, who found courage through the companionship of her beloved dog, Ruby, know that you are not alone.

Life is a journey with its twists and turns, but with the support of those who care for you, it will all be okay in the end.

May this story remind you that brighter days lie ahead and that you are stronger than you realise.

With love,
Shaz

Once upon a time, in a cosy little house on Orchard Street, Lived a little girl called Flo.

Flo had long blond hair, green eyes and a very kind heart. But her shyness made it hard for her to make friends and do things that made her nervous, like speaking in front of her class in school. This made her often feel lonely.

Flo's parents noticed her struggle and wanted to help.

But every day, Flo's anxiety would flutter like a frightened butterfly in her tummy, making her feel scared and unsure of herself.

She struggled to handle her school work and her parents couldn't bear to see her like this.

Flo's parents knew they had to find a way to help their daughter overcome her struggle and regain her confidence.

One day, Flo's parents decided to have a heart-to-heart talk with her.

They sat her down and told her that they were worried about her loneliness and shyness.

They reassured her that they loved her just the way she was, but they also wanted her to be happy and confident.

Her mum finally found a solution and she told it to her father. He said “That sounds like a wonderful idea! Bringing a furry friend into Flo's life can have many benefits and it might help her anxiety”.

Pets are known to help reduce anxiety and provide emotional support to people of all ages.

They decided to adopt a puppy for Flo but they didn’t let her know about this until they brought the little puppy home.

When the puppy arrived, her wagging tail and warm cuddles brought a huge smile to Flo's face.

Dad asked Flo what she would like to call her new friend and Flo replied without hesitation "Ruby, can I call her Ruby please Daddy?"

And so a fluffy bundle of joy named Ruby came to live with the Wyatt family. Ruby was a playful and loving puppy with soft white fur, black splodges, brown eyebrows and cheeks and deep brown eyes that shone so bright.

The Wyatt family instantly fell in love with Ruby and welcomed her into their home with open arms.

From the moment she arrived, Ruby brought a sense of happiness and excitement to everyone's lives. Flo loved her, she was so surprised and felt a sense of calmness wash over her.

Ruby sensed Flo's worries and knew just what she had to do. She would gently nudge Flo with her wet nose, as if saying, "I'm here for you. We can be brave together!"

Flo's worries started to melt away with every nudge from Ruby's wet nose. Ruby's presence was a comforting reminder that she was not alone.

Flo wrapped her arms around Ruby's furry body and whispered, "Thank you for being here, Ruby. I don't know what I would do without you my little furry friend".

One day, Flo's parents decided it was time for Ruby to go to puppy training classes where she would learn clever tricks.

Flo was worried. She didn't think she could handle the big class with lots of other people and dogs in. But Ruby nudged her and gave her a reassuring lick.

With Ruby by her side, Flo found the courage to go to the classes.

To their surprise, Flo and Ruby quickly became the stars of the class. Ruby wagged her tail, jumped through hoops, and sat obediently, while Flo beamed with pride.

The more they practiced together, the stronger their bond grew and the more fun they had together.

Flo's anxiety started to drift away as she focused on training and spending time with Ruby. The presence of her loyal companion brought a sense of calm and confidence that she had never experienced before.

With Ruby by her side, Flo felt like she could conquer any challenge that came her way.

As Flo's confidence blossomed, she and Ruby decided to enter a dog obedience competition.

Flo worked hard to train Ruby, teaching her new tricks and commands.

They practiced daily in the park, with Ruby leaping and twirling joyfully. Flo's heart swelled with happiness, knowing she was making her furry friend happy.

Finally, the big day arrived.

Flo and Ruby strutted into the competition with their heads held high. Ruby performed flawlessly, following Flo's every command.

The judges were amazed by their teamwork and awarded them first prize.

Flo's smile stretched from ear to ear, and she whispered to Ruby, "We did it, my brave little friend!"

One day, as Flo sat at her bedroom desk, anxiety crept back into her heart. She was worried about a big writing project at her school. It was a writing competition.

Remembering how Ruby had helped her before, Flo decided to write a story about their adventures together. She poured her feelings onto the pages, bringing Ruby's courage and their special bond to life.

When the school held the writing competition, Flo submitted her story.

Days later, she was called to the front of the assembly by the head teacher.

She won first prize in the competition!

The entire school cheered for Flo and Ruby's tale of bravery, and Flo's confidence soared higher than ever before.

From that day on, Flo and Ruby's friendship became a beacon of strength and love.

They continued to conquer fears together, helping others along the way. And every night, as they cuddled up together, Flo whispered to Ruby "Thank you for being my friend, my hero, and my little bundle of courage."

Ruby wagged her tail in response, as if to say, "Thank you for believing in me, Flo. Together, we can face anything."

And with that, they drifted off to sleep, ready to face a new day filled with adventures, challenges, and the unwavering bond between a little girl and her furry best friend.

Coming soon in the Adventures of Flo and Ruby

Book 2 Flo and Ruby’s remarkable journey

Book 3 Ruby's Pawsitive impact

Printed in Great Britain
by Amazon

40023003R00018